Contents

Any words appearing in the text in bold, **like this**,
are explained in the glossary.

What are textiles?

Textiles are a type of art that includes work made from materials that people weave or knit into a **fabric**. This fabric can be treated in many different ways. Some artists print onto it. Others **sculpt** the fabric or **embroider** it. This book looks at a variety of artists and **designers** who use textiles.

The birds and landscape in this piece of textile are embroidered by hand. Every colour is actually a stitch. The artist uses wool **yarns** and a needle, like a painter would use a brush and paint.

Crows by Eirian Short, 1980

RT?

KAREN HOSACK

www.raintreepublishers.co.uk
Visit our website to find out more information about Raintree books.

To order:
☎ Phone 44 (0) 1865 888112
📄 Send a fax to 44 (0) 1865 314091
💻 Visit the Raintree Bookshop at www.raintreepublishers.co.uk to browse
our catalogue and order online

Raintree is an imprint of Capstone Global Library Limited,
a company incorporated in England and Wales having its
registered office at 7 Pilgrim Street, London, EC4V 6LB
– Registered company number: 6695582

"Raintree" is a registered trademark of Pearson Education
Limited, under licence to Capstone Global Library Limited

Editorial: Adam Miller, Charlotte Guillain,
Clare Lewis and Catherine Veitch
Design: Victoria Bevan and AMR Design Ltd
Illustrations: David Woodroffe
Picture Research: Mica Brancic
Production: Victoria Fitzgerald

Originated by Dot Gradations Ltd, UK
Printed and bound by CTPS (China Translation
& Printing Services Ltd)

ISBN 978 1 4062 0941 9 (hardback)
12 11 10 09 08
10 9 8 7 6 5 4 3 2 1

ISBN 978 1 4062 0948 8 (paperback)
13 12 11 10 09
10 9 8 7 6 5 4 3 2 1

British Library Cataloguing in Publication Data
Hosack, Karen
  Textiles. - (What is art?)
  1. Textile crafts - Juvenile literature 2. Textile crafts -
  Appreciation - Juvenile literature
  I. Title
  746
A full catalogue record for this book is available from the
British Library.

Acknowledgements
The publishers would like to thank the following
for permission to reproduce photographs:
©The Bridgeman Art Library pp. **5** (Private Collection),
6 (Musee de la Tapisserie, Bayeux, France, with special
authorisation of the City of Bayeux), **10** (Ubud Market, Bali,
2002 (coloured ink on silk), Simon, Hilary (Contemporary
Artist)/Private Collection); ©Corbis/Sygma p. **21** (Bernard
Bisson); ©David Bygott & Jeannette Hanby p. **12**; ©Douglas
Atfield with permission from Freddie Robins p. **23**; ©Getty
Images p. **18** (AFP Photo/ Jean-Pierre Muller); ©Kaffe Fassett
p. **22**; ©Kyoto National Museum p. **20**; ©The Metropolitan
Museum of Art p. **26** (Purchase, Irene Lewisohn Bequest,
1961 (C.**1.81.13.1**a,b); ©The National Library of Wales p. **4**
(Eirian Short); ©The Palace Museum Bejing p. **19**; ©Courtesy
and copyright Pitt Rivers Museum, University of Oxford p. **16**;
©Polly Hope p. **8**; ©PR ShotsPrimark p. **11**; ©Rex Features
Ltd pp. **7** (Reuters/Brian Snyder), **13** (Ray Tang), **17**; ©Sarah
Jane Brown p. **24**; © Inga Liksaite / LATGA-A, Vilnius and
DACS, London, 2008 Scala Archives p. **27**; ©The State
Hermitage Museum, Russia p. **9**; ©V&A Images pp. **14**, **15**;
©World Design Inc. p. **25** (The Pomeroy Weavers, Kwa Zulu-
Natal, South Africa).

Cover photograph of Guatemala, Chichicastenango, Indian
market, embroidered fabric reproduced with permission of
Masterfile.

Every effort has been made to contact copyright holders of
any material reproduced in this book.
Any omissions will be rectified in subsequent printings if
notice is given to the publishers.

Disclaimer
All the Internet addresses (URLs) given in this book were
valid at time of going to press. However, due to the dynamic
nature of the Internet, some addresses may have changed, or
sites may have changed or ceased to exist since publication.
While the author and publishers regret any inconvenience
this may cause readers, no responsibility for any such
changes can be accepted by either the author or the
publishers. It is recommended that adults supervise children
on the Internet.

William Morris

William Morris was mainly inspired by the structures of trees and plants that he saw in nature, as well as animals. His designs for textiles were used for home furnishings, such as curtains and covers. They were also used for non-textile products like wallpaper. Fashionable people at the time filled their homes with his ideas. His aim was to bring a little bit of the outside inside. Most of these items were printed by skilled **craftspeople** using carved wooden blocks. Separate patterns, called motifs, would be designed as matching repeating images, with each colour being applied individually.

The Strawberry Thief by William Morris, 1883

William Morris was one of the most famous textile designers of the 19th Century.

Telling a story

This **medieval** length of cloth tells the story of the events of the 1066 Norman invasion of England. It is a bit like a comic strip. It is not a traditional **woven tapestry** but is actually embroidery. Like the piece on the previous page, it is created from a variety of different stitches. Some are stem stitches, which are used for the outline of the figures and the writing. Others are laid stitches, which are used for filling in the colour.

Detail from *The Bayeux Tapestry*, c.1082

The **yarn** used on The Bayeux Tapestry was **dyed** using vegetables, such as onion skins for the yellows.

Memory quilts

This quilt tells a story from more recent times. It was made to remember the victims and heroes of the terrorist attacks on the USA on September 11, 2001. Many people were involved in making the final quilt, as each individual section was added one by one. Some recognize the bravery of the emergency workers, while others show where the attacks took place, including the World Trade Center in New York.

The quilt is displayed so that people can visit it and remember those who lost their lives.

Did you know?
To make a quilt, people stitch two pieces of **fabric** together with a filling in between. Many **cultures** have used this textile method to remember people and events. Can you think of any other examples?

About a family

This textile hanging shows a family with an enormous dog and three cats. It is made from various pieces of **fabric**, some patterned, some furry, and some quilted. The large bits are used as the background wall and floor. Smaller pieces of material are layered and sewn on with a method we call **appliqué**.

Szekessy Family by Polly Hope, 1978

Each member of the family can be clearly recognized. Can you tell who the two parents are?

8

About a culture

The oldest carpet in the world was discovered in Central Asia. It is known as the Pazyryk carpet and dates from the 5th to 4th centuries BCE. It was woven with great skill which tells us that carpet-making was a respected and important trade at the time. The pictures it depicts, such as the horseman shown below, tells us how important horses were to the **culture** and day to day life.

Carpet (Detail) by Pazyryk Culture, 5th – 4th century

The ancient carpet was discovered in 1949, preserved in a layer of ice.

Ways to decorate fabric

A traditional way of decorating **fabric** is a method called **batik**. Hot wax is applied using a tool made from metal, to conduct heat. Skilled **craftspeople** make designs with the melted wax. When the wax is dry the cloth is carefully put into a dye bath. The process of drawing with wax and dying the fabric is repeated until the whole piece is covered. The wax is removed by melting it. A cracking effect happens when dye seeps into the waxed areas.

Ubud Market, Bali by Hilary Simon, 2002

This batik fabric was made in Indonesia.

This printed design uses two colours – purple and pink. The white of the t-shirt is used as the third colour for the design. It's cheaper to print using fewer colours.

Using technology

A modern way to decorate fabric is to **digitally print** images and patterns. **Designers** do this by scanning a design into a computer that is linked to a special printing machine. Using this method, people can make one-off designs as well as printing in bulk.

Pattern and symbolism

Patterns in textile designs can be **symbolic** as well as just for decoration. This means that the shapes on textiles can represent things.

These African garments are known as *kangas*. They are large pieces of printed fabric that can be worn on the body in various ways, including on the head or as a sling for carrying a baby. The patterns can include symbols such as fruit and flowers to wish for a healthy childhood, or lions or sharks to signal danger.

KINGA NA KINGA NDIPO MOTO UWAKAPO

This Kanga shows lamps, which are common in Africa. Kangas often have messages written on them. This one roughly translates as 'shelter the match and the fire will light'.

The artist Yinka Shonibare grew up in Nigeria and Britain. He has taken the idea of symbolic African *kangas* and used them to create fabric sculptures. His work celebrates the fact that different **cultures** around the world have their own traditions, and asks whether some of these traditions are being lost in the modern world.

Dysfunctional Family by Yinka Shonibare, 1999

The artist who made this sculpture grew up in a mixture of cultures. Why do you think he has made these figures look like aliens?

Fashion and pattern

Zandra Rhodes is a fashion designer who loves mixing lots of different patterns, colours, and **textures** together. In the 1960s she was famous for being too over-the-top. People thought that the colours and patterns she used did not go well together and felt that they could not wear her clothes. However, these days she is seen as a trendsetter and is highly respected in the world of fashion.

Coat by Zandra Rhodes, 1969

Do you think people would notice you if you wore a dress like this? How would you feel about standing out from the crowd?

New looks

In the 1960s, people began wearing clothes that were very different to what they had worn before. Today, we are used to seeing mini skirts, bikinis, and colourful printed fabrics, but in the 1960s these clothes were very new and daring.

It would have taken a long time to sew the beads onto this dress. They would all have been done individually by hand.

This 1920s dress is in two parts. Underneath, there is a plain white dress with a skirt. On top, a tunic shape decorates the outfit. The patterns on this 1920s dress have been carefully created using tiny beads. This makes the dress really quite heavy. In the 1920s, women would dance wearing dresses like this one. As they moved their arms and legs backwards and forwards, the dress would flap about. That is why it is called the Flapper dress.

Skill and time

It often takes a lot of skill and time to make a piece of textile. This can make the textile very special and sometimes valuable. This girl's apron was made in Sudan by a **tribal** group called Dinka Tuich. It is made of two lengths of goat's skin. One is worn on the front, and the other on the back. The thin thread which holds the sides together is also made from animal skin. The apron is decorated with tiny hand-made coloured glass beads which are put in **symmetric** patterns around the edges.

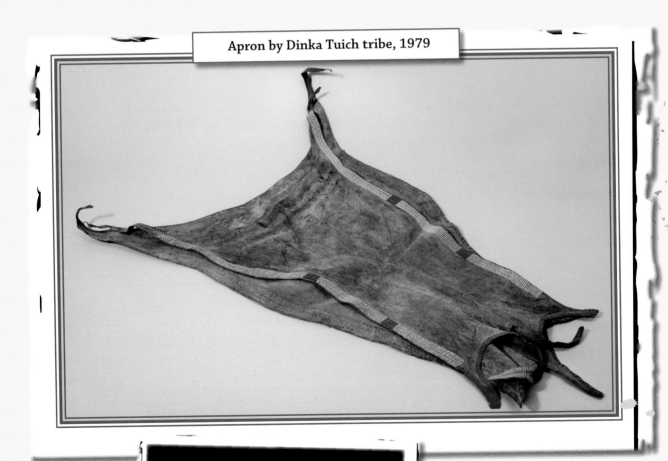

Apron by Dinka Tuich tribe, 1979

Girls would wear aprons like this to perform a special dance.

The metallic silver colour of this dress is very striking, as it catches the bright lights. This gives the dress a very modern look.

Dress by Yohji Yamamoto, 2007

Technology and geometric shapes

The Japanese fashion designer Yohji Yamamoto is famous for using **fabrics** that have been through complicated preparation. This includes **pleating**, embroidery, and other processes that use technology to press and stretch the material. The shapes of his clothes are very simple so that the main focus is on the fabric rather than other details. Because it takes so long to make one of his garments, they are very expensive.

Clothes for special occasions

Everybody likes to dress up for a special occasion. Some people are able to buy special clothes from a designer's collection. Each spring and autumn, designers from across the world show their latest clothing on **catwalks** in New York, London, Paris, and Tokyo. These clothes are usually only for individual people to order in their size. Most designers also make an 'off-the-peg' range of clothes that is not so expensive.

This dress will be quickly copied by others and more cheaply sold in high street stores days after being shown on the catwalk.

Dress by Tom Ford, 2000

On special occasions people sometimes like to wear costumes. Can you think of any costumes people put on for special events today? This picture shows a costume worn 200 years ago during the time of the Qing dynasty in China. Emperors at the time had the most talented artists working for them making these beautiful costumes from the best materials available, such as gold thread, silk, and ivory. The skirt is decorated with hundreds of handmade beads and has a pattern of crashing waves along its hem. The collar has the same beads hanging from it in a design not unlike the ceremonial chains worn by mayors today.

> On special occasions people like to wear clothes that fit the celebration.

What to wear?

What do you like wearing when you go to a family event? Are the clothes you choose different to what you wear every day? Why is this?

Ceremonial costume for Imperial Lama, Beijing, c. 18th century

Identity

Can what people wear tell us about who they are? In Japan in the Edo period (1603 to 1868) everyone knew that a woman who wore this dress was extremely wealthy and important. Each of the items that make up this twelve-layered costume has evolved in design over many centuries and can be individually named. The whole dress is made from the finest silk with hand painted designs on the back and 'kake-obi', which is worn across the shoulders.

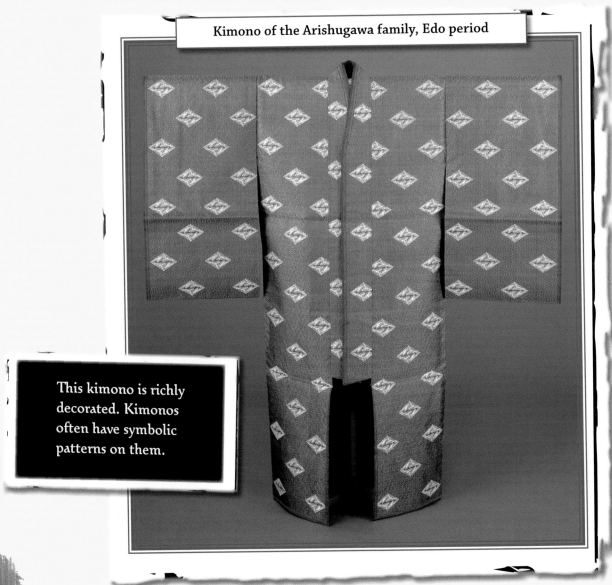

Kimono of the Arishugawa family, Edo period

This kimono is richly decorated. Kimonos often have symbolic patterns on them.

Think about it!
Do you have any clothes you wear to show your personality? What do those clothes say about you?

Do people who wear these t-shirts want to be different, or do they want to fit in with a group?

Today, people can show their **identity** through their everyday clothes. They might do this by wearing a t-shirt with the name of a band on it, or perhaps a political or environmental **slogan**. Some people try to show their personality by dressing like people they admire. Other people like to dress in a way that makes them stand out from the crowd and be seen as people with their own personal style.

Knitting

The American **designer** Kaffe Fassett visited Scotland and was inspired by the different coloured wool **yarns** there. Afterwards he decided to teach himself how to knit. The way he knits and the beautiful rich patterns and **textures** in his designs have made many people want to learn to knit, especially young people. He is most famous for his hand-knitted **commissions**, but he also designs patterns for machine-knits and weavings.

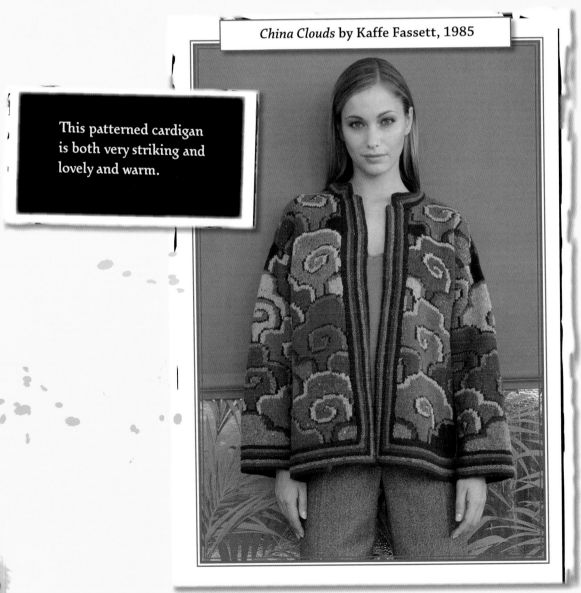

China Clouds by Kaffe Fassett, 1985

This patterned cardigan is both very striking and lovely and warm.

Needles or machine

People can knit by hand, using a pair of knitting needles, or using a machine. A machine is much faster, but knitting by hand can get more individual results.

The small details on these houses, such as the window frames, have been sewn on top of the knitting.

Knitted Homes of Crime by Freddie Robins, 2003

Knitting can be used to create sculptures too. These houses are knitted in wool. Each house is different. Some are country cottages, others are town houses. The artist selected all these houses for a specific reason that adds a message to her work. She researched the types of houses that women murderers had lived in. How does knowing this make these cosy homes seem to you now?

Unusual materials

People do not always have to knit with wool. Knitting can also be done with lots of different materials, including wire. The artist that makes these knitted wire animals uses a knitting machine. She threads the machine up in the same way as someone would if they were making a jumper or woolly hat. It is a bit more like making a wire fence instead. Once the artist has knitted a length of wire, she removes it from the machine and **moulds** it into the correct shape.

This artist has made knitted sculptures of many different animals. When they are finished they can still be moved into different shapes and positions.

Scottie Dog by Sarah Jane Brown, 2006

These baskets are made from **recycled** telephone wire. The wire has been woven together.

Gone!
Nobody can make these wire baskets any more. New technology means that the type of wire the men used is no longer available.

Basket by The Pomeroy Weavers, c.1990s

Wire baskets

These baskets were made in South Africa by men who were night watchmen in the 1990s. The men had time on their hands and knew how to make baskets. They used the waste telephone wire they found lying around the buildings they were guarding. Telephone wire is very flexible so the men developed a way of making the wire into spirals. This made it easier to work with.

Different textiles

Throughout this book we have looked at how different artists and designers from different **cultures** have used textiles in their work. We have seen how various ways of decorating and changing cloth and **yarns** can have unusual effects, and how it is possible to use a range of materials to create textile pieces.

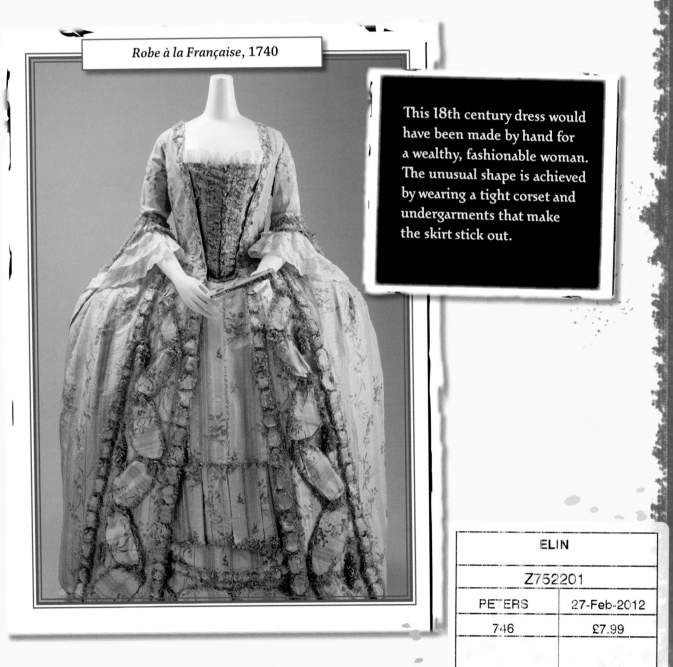

Robe à la Française, 1740

This 18th century dress would have been made by hand for a wealthy, fashionable woman. The unusual shape is achieved by wearing a tight corset and undergarments that make the skirt stick out.

Over the years, technology has changed the way that artists and designers make textiles. Artists have gone from using simple animal skins and **dyeing** processes, to more complex methods like **digital printing**. It is now possible to mix and match textile designs around the needs and interests of the person who is producing the work.

This digital image has been printed onto fabric. It could be hung on a wall as a work of art, or used to make a garment or soft furnishings.

These two examples show clearly that beautiful pieces can be created in textiles whether the artist is using modern or more traditional methods.

Timeline

Where to see textiles

This map shows where some of the textiles in this book can be seen.

① Bayeaux, Normandy, France
  The Bayeaux Tapestry

② Kent State University Museum, Ohio, USA
  Robe a la Francaise

③ London, UK
  See The William Morris Gallery for many examples of his work.

Visit the Victoria and Albert Museum to see costumes and fashion through the ages.

④ New York City, USA Metropolitan Museum: Examples of Tom Ford's work

⑤ Turkey is home to many beautiful textiles and carpets.

Glossary

appliqué sewing cut out fabric onto other fabric

batik traditional way of decorating fabric using hot wax

catwalk platform at fashion shows where models show clothes

commissions when artists are asked to produce work for money

craftspeople skilled people who make things

cultures customs of a particular time and group of people

designers people who make the plans for things that are made

digitally print way of printing using computer software

dye change the colour of a material

embroider to decorate cloth with needlework

fabric woven, knitted or felted material

identity being an individual person

medieval from the time of the Middle Ages

mould move into shape

pleating to fold and flatten fabric

recycled to convert waste into something that can be used again

sculpt make a piece of art from a solid material

slogan phrase that is easy to remember and repeat

symbolic something that represents something else

symmetric being the same on both sides

tapestry material with a woven and sometimes also embroidered design, usually hung on a wall

texture way a material feels

tribal to do with a special group or family, called a tribe

woven to make fabric by passing threads over and under each other

yarn thread used for weaving or knitting

Learn more

Books to read

Art's Alive: What are Textiles?, Ruth Thomson
(Hodder Wayland, 2007)

Stories in Art: Tapestries and Textiles, Rob Childs and
Louise Spilsbury (Hodder Wayland, 2008)

Trends in Textile Technology: Dyes and Decoration, Hazel King
(Heinemann Library, 2007)

Trends in Textile Technology: Fashion, Hazel King
(Heinemann Library, 2007)

Websites to visit

Find out about modern textile art and artists.

www.textilearts.net

Find out about the history of fashion.

www.designerhistory.com

Visit the Victoria and Albert Museum online. It has a large
collection of fashion and costumes from through the ages.

www.vam.ac.uk

Index